Professionalism Is for Everyone

Five Keys to Being
A True Professional

JAMES R. BALL

KEEP IT SIMPLE FOR SUCCESS™

Professionalism Is for Everyone:
5 Keys to Being a True Professional

ISBN: 1-887570-05-5

Copyright © 2001 James R. Ball

Published in the United States by The Goals Institute.
Printed in the United States.

Keep It Simple for Success™
is a registered trademark of The Goals Institute.

For information please contact or visit us at:

The Goals Institute
P.O. Box 3736
Reston, VA 20195-1736

www.goalsinstitute.com
www.kissbooks.com
Email: info@goalsinstitute.com

*Dedicated to
Jennifer Kuchta,
the spirit behind these books*

Welcome

HELLO!

My name is Jim Ball, and I want to welcome you on behalf of all of us at The Goals Institute and our *Keep It Simple for Success*™ team.

Congratulations! Just the fact that you have this book says a lot about you and your aspirations. *Professionalism Is for Everyone: 5 Keys to Being a True Professional* is a concise reference and guide to help you in your personal and career growth.

Professionalism really *is* for everyone. It does not matter what your job is or how much you are paid. A professional approach always stands out.

No one can guarantee success or happiness; however, I believe that the principles and concepts described here will set you apart from the crowd and give you many advantages that true professionals enjoy.

If you have any questions or comments, please drop us a note or send us an email.

If you would like additional information about our other *Keep It Simple for Success*™ books or our keynotes and seminars, please visit us at our website at www.kissbooks.com.

Best wishes for a great career!

Being a Professional

Being a professional does not guarantee that you will get the biggest office, the most important title, or the cushiest job.
It does not mean that you will make the most money or win the loudest accolades.

What being a professional does mean is that everyone will admire and respect you. They will hold you in high honor.
They will seek you out. They will want to know you, do business with you, work with you, be on your team, and be in your company.

When you are a true professional, you will always be able to look in the mirror and say:
"I like who I see; I like what I am; I am proud of what I stand for."

—Jim Ball

Contents

Professional for Life

Individuals do not become professionals because of some sudden leap that they make into the stratosphere.

Individuals become professionals because of their lifetime dedication and commitment to higher standards and ideals, honorable values, and continuous self-improvement.

—Jim Ball

Professionalism Is for Everyone

THERE IS NO SUCH THING as one job that is to be performed professionally, and another that is not.

Regardless of its size or nature, every job can be performed in a professional manner. When that happens, the individual doing the task can take pride in knowing that the work was done as well as it could be done.

Everyone admires a professional at work. It doesn't matter if you clear tables, sell insurance, design websites, deliver mail, greet customers, drive taxi, perform surgery, direct traffic, develop software, entertain in a nightclub, play tight end, paint houses, repair watches, draft wills, or minister to the ill. When you do your work professionally, people take notice.

People notice because professionals perform what often are ordinary jobs in extraordinary ways.

Professionals add a little extra to everything they do and they put a little extra into every move they make. They smile more, seem happier, act more confidently, move quicker, and take special pride in their work.

Some might argue that being professional takes too much work or is too restrictive. They may think it is easier to do just enough to get by. The problem with this is that the goal is not to get as *little* out of life as you can. The goal is to get as *much* out of life as possible.

By following the five keys in this book, you can become a true professional at whatever you do.

Remember that you are self-directed. You will reap only in proportion to what you plant. You will receive from your job only in proportion to what you contribute.

Benefits of being a professional

The greatest benefit of being a professional is the satisfaction and pride that you will enjoy from doing your work to the best of your ability. Then you will know that your work is, in fact, professional.

Another great benefit is that people will seek you out because they prefer you in comparison to the rest of the crowd.

Employers will seek you out because they know what a rarity you are in today's workforce. They will be excited about having you work for their companies.

Co-workers and friends will seek you out because they will want to be associated with you. They know they will learn from you and be inspired by you.

Customers will seek you out because the services you provide are extraordinary. They will go out of their way to make sure you are the person who helps them.

If you want true joy, choose the path of honor, pride, and self-esteem. Choose to be a professional.

The Five Keys

THESE FIVE KEYS DISTINGUISH PROFESSIONALS. Each key with its related attributes is described on the pages that follow.

1. CHARACTER is who you are and what you stand for. Professionals choose to be professional. They have integrity and they are responsible, diligent, and ethical. They do what is right and project a professional image.

2. ATTITUDE is your mental outlook. Professionals have a professional approach and a positive, serving mentality. They seek responsibility and are determined. Professionals are team players.

3. EXCELLENCE is your commitment to quality. Professionals press for excellence and continuous improvement. They are attentive and follow instructions.

4. COMPETENCY is your degree of expertise. Professionals understand their jobs and develop their skills. They produce results, perform effectively, and communicate skillfully.

5. CONDUCT is how you deal with others. Professionals are mature, polite, and loyal. They respect authority and maintain confidences. Professionals do everything with style and class.

Character

The Professional Choice

PROFESSIONALS CHOOSE TO BE PROFESSIONAL. They make a conscious decision to hold themselves to higher standards of performance and a more demanding code of conduct than most people use to guide their thoughts and actions.

When you choose to be professional, you are making a commitment to be the best that you can be and do the best that you can do in all aspects of your job, your relationships with others, and your personal development.

When you choose to be professional, you are leaving mediocrity and apathy behind. You are embarking on a lifelong journey of continual growth and the pursuit of excellence.

When you choose to be professional, you are raising the bar on the ideals you set for yourself and the demands you place upon yourself.

When you choose to be professional, you are making the best choice you can possibly make to assure your self-esteem, success, and happiness.

Dos and Don'ts

Do:

- Choose to be a professional.
- Make the commitment to continually grow.
- Set yourself apart from the crowd.
- Raise the bar on what you expect of yourself.
- Pursue a lifetime quest for excellence.
- Take pride in yourself and your work.

Don't:

- Settle for mediocrity.
- Look for the easy way.
- Expect it to be easy.

Integrity

PROFESSIONALS HAVE INTEGRITY. They understand that the foundation for all relationships is trust. They know that the four cornerstones of trust are honesty, truthfulness, forthrightness, and trustworthiness.

Honesty

When you are honest, you do not steal. Individuals who steal are dishonest and are not trusted.

Examples of dishonesty by stealing are: a shoplifter who takes a dollar pair of earrings; a construction worker who carries home tools; a food service worker who gives food to friends without charging them; a cashier who pockets money; an executive who embezzles funds.

A person does not have to actively steal something to be dishonest. An individual who knowingly receives too much change, but does not return it, is dishonest. An individual who notes an error in their favor on the restaurant bill, but does not point it out, is dishonest.

Truthfulness

When you are truthful, you tell what you believe to be the truth, the whole truth, and nothing but the truth. Individuals who do not tell the truth are liars, and are not trusted.

Examples of lying are: a job applicant who overstates his or her grades or past salary; a student who cheats on a test; an employee who calls in sick but who is not sick; a salesperson, production worker, operations manager, or customer service representative who overstates, misstates, conceals, or misrepresents facts, figures, claims, or circumstances.

Forthrightness

When you are forthright, there is a straight path between you and the truth. Individuals who are not forthright are deceptive, and are not trusted.

Examples of deception are: misconstruing facts or circumstances; leaving out important facts; exaggeration; delaying telling someone information that they should know; causing or allowing a person to accept something as true and valid that you know is not true and valid.

Trustworthiness

When you are trustworthy, you maintain confidences, you keep information confidential, and you safeguard the people and resources placed in your care. Individuals who are not trustworthy are not trusted.

Examples of untrustworthy behavior are: disclosing confidential information to third parties; abusing, squandering, destroying, or failing to protect and care for people and resources in your care.

Watch those little chinks

It takes your whole life to build your reputation, yet in the blink of an eye a single act can destroy it.

The problem with a little theft, lie, deception, or breach of confidence is that though they are little acts, they represent a chink in the armor that protects your reputation and the trust that others place in you.

An example is the employer who catches an employee padding his or her expense account with a fabricated five-dollar cab fare. Once the infraction is known, the employer will always regard the employee in a different and dimmer light.

No one is perfect. Each of us at one time or another has stolen something, lied, been deceptive, or breached a confidence. For most of us, these events occurred before we became adults and knew better.

As adults, however, not only should we know and act better, we are expected to. Character flaws and defects in any of the four cornerstones of trust cannot be tolerated in professionals because they represent a breach of trust that often is irreparable.

People want to avoid individuals who do not have integrity because they cannot be trusted.

People want to hire, work with, do business with, and be associated with individuals who have integrity because they can be trusted.

Dos and Don'ts

Do:

- Protect your integrity.
- Operate with complete honesty.
- Tell the whole truth and nothing but the truth.
- Be trustworthy.
- Be forthright and direct.

Don't:

- Underestimate the importance of your integrity.
- Steal, even a small amount.
- Lie, even a little.
- Be deceptive or misleading.
- Breach confidences that others place in you.

Being Responsible

PROFESSIONALS ARE RESPONSIBLE FOR THEIR ACTIONS AND THEIR WORK. They understand their roles and responsibilities and they are accountable for them. They discharge their duties properly, in a timely manner. They are self-starters.

Professionals can be relied on to do their job the way it is supposed to be done.

They arrive on time and frequently early. They deliver their work on time, and often ahead of schedule.

When professionals commit to doing something, they do it. They keep their word.

If, as sometimes happens, professionals make mistakes, fail to do something, or do something in error, they accept responsibility for their action and hold themselves accountable. They do not dodge blame, offer excuses, or dwell on their errors. They admit their mistakes, learn from them, and move on to the future.

Dos and Don'ts

Do:

- Accept responsibility for your actions.
- Be accountable for your roles and responsibilities.
- Be on time.
- Deliver on time.
- Keep your word.
- Admit your mistakes and learn from them.

Don't:

- Avoid or shirk responsibilities.
- Blame others or seek excuses.
- Arrive late.
- Deliver late.
- Go back on your word.
- Hide from your mistakes.

Being Diligent

PROFESSIONALS ARE DILIGENT. They pursue their tasks in a steady and earnest manner. They enjoy their work and they proceed with energy and enthusiasm.

When professionals are at work, they work. They do not spend a lot of time on personal matters. They provide a full day's effort for a full day's pay.

Dos and Don'ts

Do:

- Work when you are at work.
- Pursue your job with energy and enthusiasm.
- Get as much as possible done in the time allotted.
- Keep time for personal matters to a minimum.

Don't:

- Be a slacker, be lazy, or goof off.
- Spend a lot of time on personal calls and emails.
- Spend time on the Internet on personal matters.

Doing What Is Right

PROFESSIONALS DO WHAT IS RIGHT. They approach all individuals, situations, and circumstances with a built-in guidance system of ethics, sound judgment, fairness, equity, reasonableness, practicality, common sense, and good taste.

Professionals are generous and kind toward others. They do not take personal advantage in the negative sense of any individual, firm, organization, or situation.

Dos and Don'ts

Do:

- Say what you believe is the right thing to say.
- Do what you believe is the right thing to do.
- Be generous, kind, and fair.

Don't:

- Say anything that contradicts your values.
- Take any action that contradicts your values.
- Take advantage of anyone.
- Be unfair or unkind.

Projecting a Professional Image

PROFESSIONALS LOOK AND ACT LIKE PROFESSIONALS.
They take pride in their appearance, their posture, and
how they act.

Professionals always stand out. They look a little
cleaner, a little more polished, and a little sharper. They
appear to be more put together. They move a little faster.
They pay closer attention to details. They are more
aware of what is going on around them.

Dos and Don'ts

Do:

- Pay attention to how you look and act.
- Adopt good personal hygiene habits.
- Comb your hair and keep it neatly cut.
- Brush your teeth and take care of them.
- Keep your fingernails clean and trimmed.
- Wear clean and pressed clothes.
- Shine your shoes.
- Stand up tall, walk upright, and hold your head high.
- Move briskly.
- Keep a neat and tidy work area.

Don't:

- Let yourself go, or get careless about how you look.
- Dress sloppily or poorly.
- Wear dirty or wrinkled clothes.
- Wear chipped nail polish.
- Slouch or drag your feet.
- Make messes unless you clean them up.

Attitude

The Professional Approach

PROFESSIONALS HAVE A PROFESSIONAL APPROACH. Everything they do, they begin with an aura of confidence and quality. They are positive, enthusiastic self-starters. They take the initiative to get things going and keep them going until they are achieved.

Professionals have their share of difficulties, but when they face obstacles or sustain setbacks, they do not dwell on their misfortune. Instead, they pick themselves up, spring back, and get back on track quickly.

Professionals take responsibility for their own personal growth and development. They do what they need to do to keep current on job know-how and technologies. They have the drive to learn the skills that they require.

Dos and Don'ts

Do:

- Rise above the crowd.
- Start being a professional right now.
- Be a self-starter.
- Maintain a positive attitude.
- Express your energy and enthusiasm.
- Spring back from setbacks.
- Take responsibility for your personal development.
- Put passion into your work.
- Seek out a mentor to guide your growth.
- Be eager to learn.

Don't:

- Wait for some dream job before you start being professional.
- Wait for someone to push you or prod you along.
- Allow yourself to dwell on setbacks or obstacles.
- Assume that someone else will take care of you.

Adopting a Service Mentality

PROFESSIONALS SERVE OTHERS. They understand that service to others is the highest calling one can have. They respond by doing work that is useful and helpful. They know that serving others is one of the keys to career success, leadership opportunities, and personal reward.

Professionals see requests from customers, fellow associates, and their employers, not as a disruption to their tasks, but as an integral purpose of their work and responsibilities.

Dos and Don'ts

Do:

- Serve others.
- Do something useful and helpful.
- Be courteous, friendly, and considerate.
- Be sincere and genuine in your service.

Don't:

- Wait to be asked.
- Begrudge helping someone.
- Be patronizing or antagonistic.

Seeking Responsibility

PROFESSIONALS SEEK RESPONSIBILITY. They understand that their career progress and personal development come from stretching themselves beyond their current roles and duties.

Professionals volunteer for new assignments. They seek out opportunities to learn new skills. They welcome additional roles and responsibilities that require them to grow.

Dos and Don'ts

Do:

- Seek out and welcome new responsibilities.
- Reach for greater roles and bigger tasks.
- Stretch beyond your current duties.

Don't:

- Avoid greater responsibilities.
- Delay taking on bigger assignments.
- Be afraid to stretch and grow.

Determination

PROFESSIONALS ARE DETERMINED. Once they make a commitment to a task or goal, professionals stick to it with determination until they achieve their objective.

Professionals persist in the face of obstacles, delays, misfortunes, negative forces, and exhaustion.

Professionals are patient pursuing long-term results.

Professionals do not quit.

Dos and Don'ts

Do:

- Make the commitment to your tasks and jobs.
- Proceed with determination.
- Persist until you achieve your objectives.
- Continue with patience for long-term results.

Don't:

- Quit.
- Think about quitting.
- Get discouraged.

Being a Team Player

PROFESSIONALS ARE TEAM PLAYERS. They understand that great achievements are not won single-handedly. Great accomplishments result from the collaborative efforts of many individuals working toward common objectives and goals.

Professionals lead when they should lead. They follow when they should follow. Moreover, they are willing to do whatever task is required for the success of the team and its mission.

Professionals bolster the spirits of others with their own enthusiasm. They praise and encourage others. They give credit where credit is due.

Professionals do what they can and should do to help team members grow and participate.

Above all, professionals are loyal to their team. They take pride in their team efforts, team results, and esprit de corps.

Dos and Don'ts

Do:

- Be a willing team player.
- Do your part.
- Lead when you should lead.
- Follow when you should follow.
- Encourage and praise others.
- Take pride in your team.

Don't:

- Be a soloist.
- Be a slacker.
- Avoid leadership roles.
- Nag, complain, or be discouraging.

Excellence

Pressing for Excellence

PROFESSIONALS PRESS FOR EXCELLENCE. They strive to be the best they can be. They push to do the best work they can do.

Professionals lead the quest for excellence. They raise the bar on performance and quality. They set the pace and standards that others follow. They strive for results with the highest quality attainable consistent with the financial and time limitations involved.

Professionals complete their own work in all respects, and check it to ensure its accuracy and quality. They follow through on open items and turn in a completed product that is top quality in every way.

Professionals do not tolerate mediocrity, ever, even the smallest bit. They pay attention to details. They avoid all substandard work and performance. They take action to improve things that are not up to par.

Dos and Don'ts

Do:

- Press for excellence in all aspects of your life.
- Raise the bar and set the pace.
- Uphold the standards.
- Check your work and complete it in all respects.
- Pay attention to the details.

Don't:

- Tolerate mediocrity.
- Accept less of yourself than your standards require.
- Turn in work that is incomplete or inferior.

Continual Improvement

PROFESSIONALS CONTINUALLY IMPROVE. They constantly improve their skills and knowledge. They expand their experiences. They enhance their techniques and methods. They increase their output and quality. They add value and enlarge their usefulness in their service to others.

Professionals understand that they cannot stand still. They know that if they continue to do the same thing the same way they have been doing it, they will soon be overtaken by circumstances. Others will pass them by. They therefore put themselves on a track of continuous learning and growth.

Professionals appreciate the reality that while quantum leaps sometimes take place, improvements and innovations mostly come about by continually taking many small but steady steps over time.

Dos and Don'ts

Do:

- Become a lifelong, continual learner.
- Improve your knowledge.
- Increase your skills.
- Enhance your performance.
- Perfect your work habits.
- Take small but steady steps.

Don't:

- Wait for a quantum leap.
- Stop or slow down your learning.
- Keep on doing what you have been doing.

Being Attentive

PROFESSIONALS ARE ATTENTIVE. They listen when others are speaking. They give them the courtesy of their undivided attention. They pay attention to the matter at hand. They operate fully aware in the present. They do not let their thoughts wander.

Professionals understand that one of the great keys to their success is their ability to focus their attention on one thing at a time. While they are able to do more things at once, professionals know that doing so diminishes their effectiveness.

Professionals also know that appearing to listen while being somewhere else mentally is not only ineffective, it is rude and unprofessional. An example is the clerk who waits on a customer in person, while chatting with a co-worker or friend who is on the telephone or standing nearby.

Professionalism Is for Everyone

Dos and Don'ts

Do:

- Pay attention to the people and matters at hand.
- Do one thing at a time.
- Operate in the moment.

Don't:

- Try to perform many tasks at the same time.
- Hold multiple conversations at the same time.

Following Instructions

PROFESSIONALS FOLLOW INSTRUCTIONS. First they find out what is expected of them. Next they try to do it properly and in the time allotted.

Professionals do not alter instructions simply to exercise small personal preferences or styles.

This does not mean that professionals blindly follow instructions without thinking, for this is not the case. Professionals think independently. If professionals have been instructed to do something that is inconsistent with their values or standards or down right wrong, they will take steps to resolve those discrepancies.

Dos and Don'ts

Do:

- Follow instructions.
- Provide timely feedback on your work.
- Modify instructions you believe are inappropriate.
- Have a reason for every change.
- Make every change worthwhile.

Don't:

- Follow instructions without thinking.
- Exert unnecessary small personal preferences.
- Change things just to change things.

Competency

Expertise

PROFESSIONALS ARE EXPERTS. They understand the requirements and responsibilities of their jobs. They acquire the skills necessary to do their job properly, professionally, and with great dexterity.

Professionals realize that to become experts at what they do, they must master all aspects of their craft.

To do this, they obtain training, education, and experience. They ask questions, seek guidance, and solicit input and advice when appropriate. They are not afraid to try new things. They are willing to make mistakes in order to learn. They practice doing what they do until they are good at it.

Dos and Don'ts

Do:

- Become an expert at whatever you do.
- Learn and understand the requirements of your job.
- Acquire the training you need to do your job well.
- Practice to perfect your skills and abilities.
- Make sure you understand what is expected of you.

Don't:

- Adopt a half-hearted or apathetic approach.
- Be afraid to make mistakes or ask questions.
- Worry about being awkward while you are learning.
- Forget to practice.

Performance

PROFESSIONALS ARE TOP PERFORMERS. They know that when all is said and done, it is not desire, effort, or intentions that count, it is results.

Professionals are acutely aware of the results they are producing and the value they bring to their work and their company.

To maintain awareness of their performance, professionals record and track their progress toward improvement. They measure their output, and they continually improve the processes they use to produce it.

Dos and Don'ts

Do:

- Know the value you provide.
- Understand the results expected of you.
- Produce the greatest results you can produce.
- Record and track your output.
- Improve the processes you use to produce results.

Don't:

- Work just to put in time; work to produce results.
- Fail to record and track your progress.
- Become satisfied with current results.

Personal Effectiveness

PROFESSIONALS ARE EFFECTIVE. They understand that being efficient is good, being effective is better, and being both effective and efficient is best.

Professionals focus first on doing the right things; then they focus on doing them right.

Professionals organize themselves and their time. They adopt good work habits to optimize their efforts.

Professionals understand that time is all they have. They know where they spend their time and they spend it effectively. They make every hour of every day count. They do not waste time on non-productive activities.

Dos and Don'ts

Do:

- Focus on results.
- Develop good work habits.
- Organize your work into a logical flow.
- Create systems for repeat processes.
- Make every hour and every day count.

Don't:

- Spend time on unimportant activities.
- Fail to systematize your work.
- Diffuse your efforts.

Being a Good Communicator

PROFESSIONALS ARE GOOD COMMUNICATORS. They see effective communication as an extension of their professionalism. They recognize that knowledge and expertise are of little value until they are shared with others.

Professionals know that it is important to put their ideas across so others understand what they have to say.

Professionals do not just relate raw information, nor do they go for quantity over quality. They put information into context. They limit what they say and write to the important and relevant facts.

Professionals are brief and to the point. They use correct grammar and short, simple words.

Professionals are good listeners, too. They pay attention. They do not interrupt.

Dos and Don'ts

Do:

- Get to the main point quickly.
- Relate the facts.
- Listen when others are talking.
- Use correct grammar.
- Use short, simple words.

Don't:

- Say more than is necessary.
- Exaggerate.
- Be boring.
- Start talking just to hear yourself.
- Use a big word if a small one will do.
- Use foul language.

Conduct

Professional Maturity

PROFESSIONALS ARE MATURE. They are adults with fully developed social skills, common sense, good taste, a proper sense of timing, and an appreciation for the emotional sensibilities of others.

Professionals know how to act in any given situation. They know what to say or not say and what to do or not do. They can control their temper. They realize that anger is never an appropriate response.

Professionals can accept criticism without being defensive or argumentative.

This does not mean that professionals have lost their creative and fun-loving child aspects. Quite the contrary. Professionals laugh, have fun, and fully enjoy the lighter side of life.

Professionals work very hard, they play very hard, and they are creative. They can laugh at themselves. They enjoy casual time and good humor, and they love to have fun.

Professionals understand, however, that there is a proper time and place for everything. They mix fun and humor into their lives at the appropriate times and in the appropriate places.

Dos and Don'ts

Do:

- Find a good role model to follow.
- Act in a professional manner.
- Act with dignity.
- Use common sense and apply good taste.
- Have fun and enjoy life.
- Laugh, even at yourself.

Don't:

- Lose the child in yourself.
- Play practical jokes.
- Say or do anything that could offend others.
- Lose your temper.
- Hold a grudge.
- Get defensive or argumentative.
- Gossip or spread rumors.

Manners Matter

PROFESSIONALS USE GOOD MANNERS. They understand that good manners are an integral part of the professional persona that they possess. Good manners represent good breeding. Bad manners are rude and unprofessional.

Professionals are polite and courteous. They wait their turn. They say *please* and *thank you*. They express appreciation for the efforts of others.

Dos and Don'ts

Do:

- Be courteous and polite.
- Wait your turn.
- Say *please* and *thank you*.
- Learn and use good table manners.
- Apologize when you have offended someone.
- Thank others who do things for you.

Don't:

- Push in front of others.
- Use bad table manners.
- Forget to say *please* and *thank you*.

Loyalty

PROFESSIONALS ARE LOYAL. They understand that loyalty is an integral part of every good relationship. Professionals, therefore, operate with complete loyalty to all that they serve, work with, and depend upon.

Professionals are loyal to their family members and friends. They are loyal to their co-workers. They are loyal to their supervisors and the company they work for. They are loyal to the products, goods, and services that their company provides or represents. They are loyal to their customers and suppliers.

Dos and Don'ts

Do:

- Be loyal to your family and friends.
- Be loyal to your associates and supervisors.
- Be loyal to your company.
- Use and recommend your company's products.
- Support and stand up for others.

Don't:

- Talk negatively about anyone.
- Talk negatively about your company.
- Talk negatively about your company's products.

Respect for Authority

PROFESSIONALS RESPECT AUTHORITY. They understand that all organizations have a structure, and various individuals have roles and responsibilities to discharge. Professionals respect the positions that these individuals hold. They honor the right and responsibility of those in charge to discharge their duties.

Blind respect for authority, however, is not professional. Professionals would not allow the authority of others if to do so would be incongruent with their own good judgment, standards, or code of conduct.

Dos and Don'ts

Do:

- Respect the authority of others.

Don't:

- Undermine the authority of others.
- Do anything that you believe is inappropriate.
- Do anything that you believe is illegal or immoral.
- Act contrary to your values or standards.

Confidences and Confidentiality

PROFESSIONALS KEEP CONFIDENCES. They keep information confidential. Professionals understand that any breach of confidence or confidential information is a breach of trust.

Professionals operate with the highest standards possible to maintain confidences and to keep proprietary and confidential information confidential.

Professionals take care to avoid idle talk in public places such as elevators and restaurants, where they may be observed or overheard.

Dos and Don'ts

Do:

- Keep confidences.
- Keep information confidential.
- Respect the privacy of others.

Don't:

- Discuss confidential information in public places.
- Give confidential information to third parties.
- Eavesdrop.
- Gossip.

A Touch of Class

PROFESSIONALS HAVE CLASS. They know that there is a difference between just doing things and doing things in style. They show elegance and taste in tangible objects, in the way they conduct themselves, and in the environments they create.

Class and style are not shown through lavish expenditures or adornments, but rather by exquisite attention to quality and details, and by doing just the right thing at just the right time. A simple thank you note on quality stationery is much better than an impersonal email. The email may get the job done, but the carefully written note demonstrates class.

Dos and Don'ts

Do:

- Develop your own unique sense of style and class.
- Pay attention to the details.
- Turn ordinary events into extraordinary occasions.

Don't:

- Settle for the ordinary.
- Fake sincerity or quality.

Ten Commandments of Professionalism

1. *Thou shalt make a commitment to being a professional.*

2. *Thou shalt always do and say what you believe is the right thing to do or say.*

3. *Thou shalt look and act professionally.*

4. *Thou shalt take pride in your work.*

5. *Thou shalt learn your craft and teach it to others.*

6. *Thou shalt be accountable and responsible for your actions.*

7. *Thou shalt not tolerate mediocrity.*

8. *Thou shalt do whatever you need to do whenever you need to do it.*

9. *Thou shalt do something useful to serve others.*

10. *Thou shalt not be a hack.*

Note: The tenth commandment above is from Robert Mckee's screenwriting course, *Story*.

About the Author

JAMES R. BALL is CEO of The Goals Institute, a company that helps businesses and organizations achieve their potential through goal achievement.

Through The Goals Institute, Mr. Ball provides executive development programs and keynote speeches for corporations and organizations. He also is a co-creator of the *Keep It Simple for Success*™ series and has written or co-written several of these books.

Mr. Ball previously was the co-founder and CEO of a venture capital firm that helped launch more than twenty companies including The Discovery Channel. Before that, he was a managing partner at Arthur Andersen in charge of an office that served high technology companies.

He has been an adjunct faculty member at George Mason University where he co-founded George Mason University Entrepreneurial Institute, Inc.

Mr. Ball is a certified public accountant and a member of the American Institute of Certified Public Accountants. He and his wife Dolly live in Virginia. They have two daughters, Jennifer and Stephanie.

Also by Jim Ball

Soar . . . If You Dare®
DNA Leadership through Goal-Driven Management
The Entrepreneur's Tool Kit
ABCs for Life

If you work for a man,
in heaven's name, work for him!

Speak well of him, think well of him
and stand by the Institution he represents.

—Elbert Hubbard

Best wishes for
great success and happiness!

IF YOU WOULD LIKE more information about our other
Keep It Simple for Success titles, our discounts for
volume purchases, our speaking and leadership seminar
services, or would like to send us your comments or
suggestions, please contact or visit us at:

The Goals Institute
P.O. Box 3736
Reston, VA 20195-1736

www.goalsinstitute.com
www.kissbooks.com
Email: info@goalsinstitute.com

Professionalism Is for Everyone